What Does the
PRINCIPAL
Do?

Rita Kidde

PowerKiDS press
New York

Published in 2015 by The Rosen Publishing Group, Inc.
29 East 21st Street, New York, NY 10010

First Edition

Editor: Amelie von Zumbusch
Book Design: Colleen Bialecki
Photo Research: Katie Stryker

Photo Credits: Cover Mark Bowden/E+/Getty Images; cover (background) shooarts/Shutterstock.com; p. 5 Jupiterimages/Stockbyte/Thinkstock; p. 6 Fuse/Getty Images; p. 9 Jose Luis Pelaez Inc/Blend Images/Getty Images; p. 10 Hero Images/Getty Images; p. 13 Michaeljung/iStock/Thinkstock; p. 14 Image Source/Getty Images; p. 17 Jack Hollingsworth/Digital Vision/Thinkstock; p. 18 Fuse/Thinkstock; p. 21 Echo/Cultura/Getty Images; p. 22 Jupiterimages/Pixland/Thinkstock.

Publisher's Cataloging Data

Kidde, Rita.
What does the principal do? / by Rita Kidde. — 1st ed. — New York : PowerKids Press, c2015
        p. cm. — (Jobs in my school)
Includes an index.
ISBN: 978-1-4777-6477-0 (Library Binding)
ISBN: 978-1-4777-6534-0 (Paperback)
ISBN: 978-1-4777-6537-1 (6-pack)
1. School principals—Juvenile literature. 2. School management and organization—Juvenile literature.   I. Title.
LB2831.9.K57 2015
371.2'012

Manufactured in the United States of America

CPSIA Compliance Information: Batch # WS14PK4: For Further Information contact Rosen Publishing, New York, New York at 1-800-237-9932

CONTENTS

Principals run schools. Do you know your principal?

In some schools, the principal is called the head or headmaster.

The **teachers** report to the principal. The principal reports to the superintendent.

There are more than 200,000 principals in the United States.

Most principals were once teachers. They like to work with kids.

Principals go to a lot of **meetings**. They meet with teachers. They meet with parents.

They hire teachers. They help train new teachers.

The principal helps set the school budget. This controls how money is spent.

When kids act up, they get sent to the principal's office.

If you need help, go to the principal. She will be happy to help you!

WORDS TO KNOW

meeting

principal

teacher

WEBSITES

Due to the changing nature of Internet links, PowerKids Press has developed an online list of websites related to the subject of this book. This site is updated regularly. Please use this link to access the list: www.powerkidslinks.com/josc/prin/

INDEX